VIOLA

2ND EDITION

THE BEST OF
The Beatles

T0085241

ISBN 978-1-4234-1048-5

HAL•LEONARD®
CORPORATION
7777 W. BLUEMOUND RD. P.O. BOX 13819 MILWAUKEE, WI 53213

Visit Hal Leonard Online at
www.halleonard.com

CONTENTS

ALL MY LOVING

VIOLA

Words and Music by JOHN LENNON
and PAUL McCARTNEY

ACROSS THE UNIVERSE

VIOLA

Words and Music by JOHN LENNON
and PAUL McCARTNEY

Slowly and smoothly

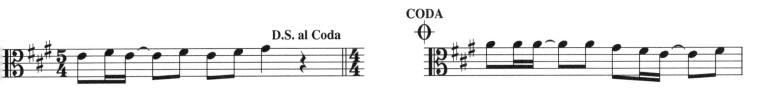

ALL YOU NEED IS LOVE

VIOLA

Words and Music by JOHN LENNON
and PAUL McCARTNEY

AND I LOVE HER

IOLA

Words and Music by JOHN LENNON
and PAUL McCARTNEY

BACK IN THE U.S.S.R.

VIOLA

Words and Music by JOHN LENNON
and PAUL McCARTNEY

THE BALLAD OF JOHN AND YOKO

VIOLA

Words and Music by JOHN LENNON
and PAUL McCARTNEY

Moderate Rock

BECAUSE

VIOLA

Words and Music by JOHN LENNON
and PAUL McCARTNEY

BIRTHDAY

VIOLA

Words and Music by JOHN LENNON
and PAUL McCARTNEY

Moderately fast Rock

BLACKBIRD

VIOLA

Words and Music by JOHN LENNON
and PAUL McCARTNEY

CAN'T BUY ME LOVE

VIOLA

Words and Music by JOHN LENNON
and PAUL McCARTNEY

COME TOGETHER

VIOLA

Words and Music by JOHN LENNO
and PAUL McCARTNE

Slowly

A DAY IN THE LIFE

IOLA

Words and Music by JOHN LENNON
and PAUL McCARTNEY

DAY TRIPPER

VIOLA

Words and Music by JOHN LENNON
and PAUL McCARTNEY

DEAR PRUDENCE

IOLA

Words and Music by JOHN LENNON
and PAUL McCARTNEY

DO YOU WANT TO KNOW A SECRET?

VIOLA

Words and Music by JOHN LENNON
and PAUL McCARTNEY

Slowly and freely

Moderately

To Coda

D.S. al Coda

CODA

DRIVE MY CAR

IOLA

Words and Music by JOHN LENNON
and PAUL McCARTNEY

Moderately, with a beat

EIGHT DAYS A WEEK

VIOLA

Words and Music by JOHN LENNON
and PAUL McCARTNEY

Moderately

ELEANOR RIGBY

VIOLA

Words and Music by JOHN LENNON
and PAUL McCARTNEY

Moderately

EVERY LITTLE THING

VIOLA

Words and Music by JOHN LENNON
and PAUL McCARTNEY

THE FOOL ON THE HILL

VIOLA

Words and Music by JOHN LENNON
and PAUL McCARTNEY

FROM ME TO YOU

VIOLA

Words and Music by JOHN LENNON
and PAUL McCARTNEY

Moderately

GET BACK

VIOLA

Words and Music by JOHN LENNON
and PAUL McCARTNEY

Moderately

GIRL

VIOLA

Words and Music by JOHN LENNON
and PAUL McCARTNEY

GOLDEN SLUMBERS

IOLA

Words and Music by JOHN LENNON
and PAUL McCARTNEY

GOOD DAY SUNSHINE

VIOLA

Words and Music by JOHN LENNO
and PAUL McCARTNE

Moderately

To Coda ⊕

1.

2. 3.

D.C. al Coda   CODA ⊕

GOT TO GET YOU INTO MY LIFE

VIOLA

Words and Music by JOHN LENNON
and PAUL McCARTNEY

Very steady (not too fast) ($\sqcap$ = $\overset{3}{\overline{}}$)

A HARD DAY'S NIGHT

VIOLA

Words and Music by JOHN LENNON
and PAUL McCARTNEY

HELLO, GOODBYE

VIOLA

Words and Music by JOHN LENNON
and PAUL McCARTNEY

HELP!

VIOLA

Words and Music by JOHN LENNON
and PAUL McCARTNEY

HELTER SKELTER

VIOLA

Words and Music by JOHN LENNON
and PAUL McCARTNEY

HERE COMES THE SUN

VIOLA

Words and Music
GEORGE HARRISON

HERE, THERE AND EVERYWHERE

VIOLA

Words and Music by JOHN LENNON
and PAUL McCARTNEY

Moderately slow

HEY JUDE

VIOLA

Words and Music by JOHN LENNON
and PAUL McCARTNEY

I FEEL FINE

Words and Music by JOHN LENNON
and PAUL McCARTNEY

I AM THE WALRUS

VIOLA

Words and Music by JOHN LENNON
and PAUL McCARTNEY

I SAW HER STANDING THERE

VIOLA

Words and Music by JOHN LENNON
and PAUL McCARTNEY

Moderately bright, with a beat

I SHOULD HAVE KNOWN BETTER

Words and Music by JOHN LENNON
and PAUL McCARTNEY

VIOLA

I WANT TO HOLD YOUR HAND

VIOLA

Words and Music by JOHN LENNO
and PAUL McCARTNE

Moderately

I WILL

Words and Music by JOHN LENNON
and PAUL McCARTNEY

VIOLA

I'LL CRY INSTEAD

VIOLA

Words and Music by JOHN LENNON
and PAUL McCARTNEY

Brightly

I'LL FOLLOW THE SUN

OLA

Words and Music by JOHN LENNON
and PAUL McCARTNEY

Moderately

I'M A LOSER

VIOLA

Words and Music by JOHN LENNON
and PAUL McCARTNEY

Moderately

I'M HAPPY JUST TO DANCE WITH YOU

VIOLA

Words and Music by JOHN LENNON
and PAUL McCARTNEY

Moderately

I'VE JUST SEEN A FACE

VIOLA

Words and Music by JOHN LENNO
and PAUL McCARTNE

Brightly, in 2

IF I FELL

VIOLA

Words and Music by JOHN LENNON
and PAUL McCARTNEY

IN MY LIFE

VIOLA

Words and Music by JOHN LENNON
and PAUL McCARTNEY

IT WON'T BE LONG

Words and Music by JOHN LENNON
and PAUL McCARTNEY

VIOLA

IT'S ONLY LOVE

VIOLA

Words and Music by JOHN LENNON
and PAUL McCARTNEY

Moderately

JULIA

VIOLA

Words and Music by JOHN LENNON
and PAUL McCARTNEY

LADY MADONNA

VIOLA

Words and Music by JOHN LENNON
and PAUL McCARTNEY

LET IT BE

VIOLA

Words and Music by JOHN LENNON
and PAUL McCARTNEY

THE LONG AND WINDING ROAD

VIOLA

Words and Music by JOHN LENNON
and PAUL McCARTNEY

Slowly

LOVE ME DO

VIOLA

Words and Music by JOHN LENNON
and PAUL McCARTNEY

Moderate Shuffle

LUCY IN THE SKY WITH DIAMONDS

VIOLA

Words and Music by JOHN LENNON
and PAUL McCARTNEY

MAGICAL MYSTERY TOUR

VIOLA

Words and Music by JOHN LENNON
and PAUL McCARTNEY

MARTHA MY DEAR

Words and Music by JOHN LENNON
and PAUL McCARTNEY

VIOLA

MICHELLE

VIOLA

Words and Music by JOHN LENNON
and PAUL McCARTNEY

NO REPLY

VIOLA

Words and Music by JOHN LENNON
and PAUL McCARTNEY

NORWEGIAN WOOD
(This Bird Has Flown)

VIOLA

Words and Music by JOHN LENNON
and PAUL McCARTNEY

Slowly

NOWHERE MAN

VIOLA

Words and Music by JOHN LENNON
and PAUL McCARTNEY

OB-LA-DI, OB-LA-DA

VIOLA

Words and Music by JOHN LENNON
and PAUL McCARTNEY

OCTOPUS'S GARDEN

VIOLA

Words and Music by RICHARD STARKEY
JOHN LENNON and PAUL McCARTNEY

PAPERBACK WRITER

VIOLA

Words and Music by JOHN LENNON
and PAUL McCARTNEY

Bright Rock

PENNY LANE

VIOLA

Words and Music by JOHN LENNON
and PAUL McCARTNEY

PLEASE PLEASE ME

VIOLA

Words and Music by JOHN LENNON
and PAUL McCARTNEY

Moderately

P.S. I LOVE YOU

VIOLA

Words and Music by JOHN LENNON
and PAUL McCARTNEY

REVOLUTION

VIOLA

Words and Music by JOHN LENNON
and PAUL McCARTNEY

Moderate Rock and Roll Shuffle

RUN FOR YOUR LIFE

Words and Music by JOHN LENNON
and PAUL McCARTNEY

VIOLA

Moderately

SGT. PEPPER'S LONELY HEARTS CLUB BAND

VIOLA

Words and Music by JOHN LENNON
and PAUL McCARTNEY

SHE LOVES YOU

VIOLA

Words and Music by JOHN LENNON
and PAUL McCARTNEY

SHE'S A WOMAN

Viola

Words and Music by JOHN LENNON
and PAUL McCARTNEY

SOMETHING

VIOLA

Words and Music by
GEORGE HARRISON

STRAWBERRY FIELDS FOREVER

VIOLA

Words and Music by JOHN LENNON
and PAUL McCARTNEY

TELL ME WHY

VIOLA

Words and Music by JOHN LENNON
and PAUL McCARTNEY

THANK YOU GIRL

VIOLA

Words and Music by JOHN LENNON
and PAUL McCARTNEY

THINGS WE SAID TODAY

VIOLA

Words and Music by JOHN LENNON
and PAUL McCARTNEY

THIS BOY
(Ringo's Theme)

VIOLA

Words and Music by JOHN LENNON
and PAUL McCARTNEY

Slow Rock & Roll

TICKET TO RIDE

VIOLA

Words and Music by JOHN LENNON
and PAUL McCARTNEY

TWIST AND SHOUT

VIOLA

Words and Music by BERT RUSSELL
and PHIL MEDLEY

WE CAN WORK IT OUT

VIOLA

Words and Music by JOHN LENNON
and PAUL McCARTNEY

WHEN I'M SIXTY-FOUR

Words and Music by JOHN LENNON
and PAUL McCARTNEY

VIOLA

WHILE MY GUITAR GENTLY WEEPS

VIOLA

Words and Music by
GEORGE HARRISON

WITH A LITTLE HELP FROM MY FRIENDS

VIOLA

Words and Music by JOHN LENNON
and PAUL McCARTNEY

THE WORD

VIOLA

Words and Music by JOHN LENNON
and PAUL McCARTNEY

Moderately

YELLOW SUBMARINE

VIOLA

Words and Music by JOHN LENNON
and PAUL McCARTNEY

YES IT IS

VIOLA

Words and Music by JOHN LENNON
and PAUL McCARTNEY

YESTERDAY

Words and Music by JOHN LENNON
and PAUL McCARTNEY

VIOLA

Moderately

YOU CAN'T DO THAT

VIOLA

Words and Music by JOHN LENNON
and PAUL McCARTNEY

YOU WON'T SEE ME

Words and Music by JOHN LENNON
and PAUL McCARTNEY

VIOLA

YOU'RE GOING TO LOSE THAT GIRL

VIOLA

Words and Music by JOHN LENNON
and PAUL McCARTNEY

YOU'VE GOT TO HIDE YOUR LOVE AWAY

VIOLA

Words and Music by JOHN LENNON
and PAUL McCARTNEY

Moderately

YOUR MOTHER SHOULD KNOW

VIOLA

Words and Music by JOHN LENNON
and PAUL McCARTNEY